Sermon

on the

Mount

by

John D. Mummert

RAGGED EDGE PRESS

This Ragged Edge Press publication
was printed by
Beidel Printing House, Inc.
63 West Burd Street
Shippensburg, PA 17257-0152 USA

In respect for the scholarship contained herein, the acid-free paper used in this book meets the guidelines for permanence and durability of the Committee on Production Guidelines for Book Longevity of the Council on Library Resources.

For a complete list of available publications
please write
Ragged Edge Press
Division of White Mane Publishing Company, Inc.
P.O. Box 152
Shippensburg, PA 17257-0152 USA

Library of Congress Cataloging-in-Publication Data

Mummert, John D., 1948–
        Sermon on the mount / by John D. Mummert.
            p.   cm.
        Includes bibliographical references.
        ISBN 1-57249-146-9 (alk. paper)
        1. Sermon on the mount--Criticism, interpretation, etc.
    I. Title.
    BT380.2.M75
    241.5'3--dc21
                                                                    98-42235
                                                                        CIP

PRINTED IN THE UNITED STATES OF AMERICA

Dedication

To my wife, Regena, and my children, Peter, Sarah, Anne, Jeremy, and Matthew

Contents

Preface

The disagreement started during a Bible study session I taught. I was explaining that Christianity requires that we follow Jesus, not merely with our minds, but with our actions and will as well. "Faith is more than intellectual belief," I said. "It is intended to be a total response of our lives to the claims of Jesus Christ. Jesus wants to be both our Savior and our Lord."

An interruption caught me off guard. "We are saved simply by faith in Jesus Christ," claimed a man, without even waiting to be recognized. "My Bible says in Ephesians 2:8 'For it is by grace you have been saved, through faith.'" Although he and I carried on a vigorous discussion, we did not reconcile our differences that night—or ever. The man and his wife left my congregation, causing me to relive that exchange in my mind countless times.

That incident, in fact, became the motivating force for this book. My purpose in writing is to deal with the most central and fundamental question of Christianity: How does Christ want us to live? Having reflected on this issue, I created the following criteria for an answer: the primary direction must come from the words of Christ himself, and the validity of the direction must be confirmed by the life habits of the early Christians, those who were closest to Christ's message and who knew of it firsthand or lived within the immediate several generations following Christ. It is reasonable to assume that Christ's disciples and those whom they taught would have understood his intentions and would have attempted to live by his words.

The first question becomes: which of Christ's teachings are paramount? The answer comes from Jesus himself, words taken from Matthew 7:24 which refer to the Sermon on the Mount. "Therefore anyone who hears these words of mine and puts them into practice is like a wise man who built his house on a rock." The figure of speech that Christ selected demonstrates that he considers his words in the Sermon on the Mount to be a "solid foundation" for living, a guide not merely for understanding but for action. The Sermon on the Mount, found in Matthew 5 to 7, is one of the most quoted sections of the New Testament. Even those with only a vague knowledge of the Bible are usually familiar with the teachings of the Sermon on the Mount. The Beatitudes are found there, as is the Lord's Prayer. The Sermon on the Mount contains familiar words about loving our enemies, practical advice about not judging others, and helpful words about trusting in the Lord. Christians should share a common understanding and belief in these practices.

If by definition, a Christian is one who accepts Christ's salvation and the inspired nature of Scripture, then he is exhorted by Christ himself to live by the words contained in the Sermon on the Mount. Because the Sermon on the Mount is central to the Christian message, it deserves to be studied carefully as a guide to living in a truly Christian manner. This book will gloss passages from the Sermon on the Mount and pair them with excerpts from the writings of the early church authors in order to demonstrate that the Sermon on the Mount formed the morality and ethics of the early Christian church.

Introduction

By exploring writing from the early Christian church one can conclude that Christ intended his message from the Sermon on the Mount to be a model of living. The early Christians lived and obeyed the words of the Sermon on the Mount. Although they may not have had access to a complete collection of the books and letters that make up our New Testament— for the canonical works had not yet been defined—the early Christians built their beliefs upon a combination of texts and oral tradition, often consisting of the words of Jesus.

The works of the Ante-Nicene writers—those who wrote before the first Council of Nicea in 325 A.D.—contain a strong ethical and moral flavor, with far more quotations coming from the Sermon on the Mount than any other passage of the Scriptures. It is easy to understand why this is so; some of the writers, Clement of Rome and Ignatius of Antioch for example, were companions of the apostles and obviously would have heard of the Sermon on the Mount from those who witnessed Christ preaching it. What sort of effect did this proximity to Christ's message have? Many of the early Christian writers were martyred for their faith in Christ, oftentimes accepting brutal torture and murder when the slightest denial—even a token one— could have set them free. No one can study their writings without developing a profound respect for the deep faith of those who risked and gave all to be true to Christ. From their own words, we can conclude that the early Christians did not debate whether or not they should obey the Sermon on the Mount; they alluded to it and lived it!

The Early Christians

Who were these early Christians, those who learned of Christ from his apostles and disciples? Sadly, most of us know little about them. We are aware of the book of Acts, but beyond that lies a huge, mysterious gap to most Protestants, whose awareness of religious history picks up with the reformation and Martin Luther. To understand early Christianity, we must move beyond the book of Acts and focus on the writers who lived during the early Christian era, from roughly 90 A.D. to the Council of Nicea in 325 A.D. The Apostle John was still living at the beginning of this period, and the apostles themselves taught the first generation of these writers. These leaders of the early church knew biblical Greek intimately and lived the culture of the New Testament. Collectively, they formed a far-reaching community and maintained bonds of fellowship and communion with each other. These men were godly men, pastors of the early churches, and guardians of the apostolic faith. One can understand them by referencing the quotation from II Timothy 2:2, that truth was entrusted "to faithful men, who will be able to teach others also."

It is important to distinguish these writers from the early heretical writers. At the end of the first century and the beginning of the second, many false writings about Christ were produced, the so-called apocryphal writings. Even though these false writings sometimes carried the names of the apostles, it is generally easy to identify their apocryphal nature because of the fanciful and legendary nature of the stories about the childhood of Christ, the life of the Virgin Mary, and the activities of the apostles.

Orthodox Christian writers who had to contend with these false teachings defended the true faith. The result of their struggle was the production of the theology of the apologists—those who perpetuated the original gospel of Christ. During this period, the church began to establish which writings belonged to the Scripture and which did not, their decision being based an the genuine apostolic testimony in the writings.

Sometimes the early Christian writers are called "fathers" of the church. While the title bestows well-deserved respect for their primacy, these men saw themselves simply as Christian leaders and workers. They did not write formal theological treatises. Their writings fall into several categories: (1) Apologetic works which explained to the Romans and Jews universally held Christian beliefs; (2) Works defending apostolic Christianity against heretics; and (3) Correspondence between churches which dealt with practical and moral issues. These writings reveal what the early Christians professed in the period after the apostles died, which makes them invaluable as spiritual guides.

A Brief Sketch of Early Christianity

While the reader may turn to the appendix for biographical sketches on the early Christian writers, let us begin with a brief overview of the early church to understand the commitment that was necessary to be a true follower of Christ. We can gain an immediate appreciation of the hostility with which Christianity was met by realizing that three of the most famous early Christian leaders—Ignatius of Antioch (d. 110), Polycarp of Smyrna (d. 156), and the philosopher Justin (d. 165)—all were martyred for their faith. In fact, for the major portion of the second century, Roman imperial authorities persecuted the church as an "illegal religion." In the eyes of the Romans, Christians were criminals, not only religiously, but politically. Their crime was that they refused to honor the earthly emperor as king, lord, and god as was required of them as members of imperial society. The persecution of Christians in the second century was largely local, conducted with zeal by the local imperial authorities. Nevertheless, the persecutions were widespread and Christians were generally hated even by the most tolerant and open-minded of the Roman rulers.

The Christian church lived in relative peace from the death of Marcus Aurelius (d. 185) to the reign of the emperor Decius (d. 249). When Decius came to power, he inaugurated a persecution of Christians throughout the whole empire. The clergy were targeted for death, and all Christian property was to be confiscated or destroyed. An all-out attempt was made to purge the church of its leadership and destroy it completely.

The third century brought interior crisis to the church as well. The question arose about what to do with those Christians who denied Christ under the threat of torture and execution, and who lapsed from Christian life into sin in times of peace. A number of schisms in the church caused some of the faithful to leave the church for what they considered a more pure and rigorous form of Christianity. Tertullian, the great father of Latin theology, was among them.

The great defender of the church during this time was Cyprian, the bishop of Carthage (d. 258), who himself died a martyr's death. The third century also saw the emergence of the first formal school of Christian theology. It was located in Alexandria, Egypt, and was developed by Clement of Alexandria.

Writings in the third century give insight into the worship and practices of the church, specifically *The Teachings of the Twelve Apostles* from Syria and *The Apostolic Tradition* of Hippolytus of Rome (d. 235) who wrote in Greek. These texts offer regulations for those in church offices and tell of worship forms.

The fourth century began with the greatest persecution ever waged against the early church, that of Diocletian. However, in 312 A.D., an important shift took place. Constantine, who was about to engage in battle with his rival Maxentius, had a vision of the cross with the words, "In this sign, conquer," inscribed on it. He placed the Christian symbol on his troops' tunics and weapons. When his army was victorious, Constantine quickly moved to grant freedom to Christians to practice their faith openly.

The First Ecumenical Council was held in Nicea in 325 A.D., with Christian leaders coming from all parts of the empire. This council made creedal affirmations that we still follow today. By 380 A.D. Christianity became the official religion of the empire by decree of the emperor Theodosius. The young church, which had endured centuries of persecution while following Christ's lead, emerged as the central religious force in the Western world.

The Historical Shift

It remains for us to consider how, down through the ages, Christians have drifted away from the clear discipleship of the Sermon on the Mount. The comments that follow are not meant to condemn, but to point out how and why over the last two thousand years interpretations of the Sermon on the Mount have changed. The renowned theologians who are responsible for the shift have mostly held orthodox convictions; they share a common commitment to the message of God's eternal love and Christ's sacrifice on the Cross. Furthermore, we believe deeply that Jesus' most profound and forgiving teaching should not be turned into narrow and legalistic outward rules.

The question remains: What happened to the Sermon on the Mount? How have Christ's words, so explicit and clear, come to be misunderstood? To answer this question, let us briefly review how various influential Christian writers and theologians have treated the Sermon on the Mount. This thumbnail historical sketch will help us understand how Christians have drifted away from the original intention of Christ's own words in the Sermon on the Mount.

Augustine, Bishop of Hippo

One of the first Christians to write an extensive commentary on the Sermon on the Mount—two volumes, in fact—was St. Augustine in the fourth century. Augustine viewed the Sermon as the "perfect measure of the Christian life,"[1] but he also argued that you couldn't take all of the teaching of the Sermon on the Mount in a literal way. So, for example, he developed a "just war" theory. He also believed there was a tension between the demands of Jesus' law and the law of the Old Testament. With Augustine, a slow erosion of commitment to a literal acceptance of the Sermon on the Mount began.

Thomas Aquinas

Thomas Aquinas (1225–1274) in his *Summa Theologica* not only laid the foundation for modern Catholic theology, but also had a profound indirect influence on Protestant theology. He distinguished between "precepts" and "evangelical counsels" in the Sermon on the Mount.[2] A "precept" was an obligation, while a "counsel" was optional. Aquinas taught a law of liberty regarding the moral and ethical teachings of the Sermon on the Mount, in effect, arguing that a Christian could pick and choose what to obey. Aquinas' theology represents a profound change from the words of Jesus and the teachings of the early church. Christians have been plagued with this alteration ever since.

Martin Luther

Martin Luther (1483–1546) inspired the Protestant Reformation. His writings on the Sermon on the Mount consisted of a series of sermons, later developed into a commentary. Luther's concern with the "enthusi-asts," or Anabaptists, informed his commentary. He argued that they con-fused the "secular" with the "spiritual," the "kingdom of the world" with the "kingdom of Christ." Luther, therefore, developed a "two-kingdom" approach in the Sermon on the Mount.[3] If you were unable to carry out the demand for obedience, you would simply trust God's grace for salvation. In his post-script to the Sermon on the Mount, Luther contrasted grace and works, seeing them as opposed. Luther argued that the corrupt "papists" taught the importance of "works of righteousness."

John Calvin

John Calvin (1509–1564), another key reformer, treated the Sermon on the Mount in his famous work, the *Institutes of the Christian Religion*. He believed in predestination so he argued that salvation was totally the work of God. Since an individual was predestined to be either saved or damned, living by the Sermon on the Mount became superfluous. Good works couldn't save a soul if salvation wasn't part of God's plan. Being a Pharisee who "focused on external obedience" would not help either.

Anabaptism

The Anabaptists, sometimes called the "left-wing" of the reformation, sought a more radical reformation than Martin Luther or John Calvin. The Anabaptists reformed moral and ethical teachings as well as doctrine. They sought to "restore" New Testament Christianity, rather than simply "reform" doctrine. The Anabaptists were concerned with outward actions and in-ward faith. A Christian's life was to be holy and obedient. In some ways, Anabaptism resembled early Christianity.

The Anabaptists believed it was possible to establish a holy church consisting of real disciples, Christians who would separate themselves from the world by following Jesus' teachings in the Sermon on the Mount. Be-lieving in a strict separation of church and state, they avoided oaths, re-fused to serve in the military, and had a deep concern for society's outcasts. Despite their literal interpretation of the Sermon on the Mount, even the Anabaptists have had their divisions through the years.

Dispensationalism

Many evangelicals today have been influenced by dispensationalism, popularized by the American congregationalist Cyrus T. Scofield in *The Scofield Reference Bible*. Classic dispensationalism teaches that the Ser-mon on the Mount does not apply to present day Christians. Rather, Christ intended it to apply to a future "kingdom" or a "millennial age."

We can see this idea influencing other Christian writers. *Unger's Bible Handbook* says of Matthew, "Since this Gospel is Jewish, the key to the interpretation of Matthew is an understanding of God's program of Israel and her Messiah. This involves the great focal point of Israel's future under the Messiah."[4] Charles Larkin, whose charts and books are still available in Christian bookstores, wrote that the teachings of the Sermon on the Mount "have no application to the Christian, but only to those under the Law, and therefore must apply to another Dispensation than this."[5] Lewis Sperry Chafin, the founder of the Dallas Theological Seminary, asserted that the Sermon on the Mount had no application to either the concept of salvation or grace. Its purpose was to declare "the essential character of the millennial kingdom."[6]

A Challenge

It has been said that the Sermon on the Mount will lead us either to transformation or despair. Robert Frost summed up this conflict when he said, "The Sermon on the Mount is just a frame-up to insure the failure of us all, so all of us will be thrown prostrate at the mercy seat for mercy." Frost also called the Sermon on the Mount "irresistible beauty no one can live up to."[7] Perhaps Augustine, Aquinas, Luther, Calvin, and the dispensationalists all had similar feelings in backing away from the message of the Sermon on the Mount. To some extent, all these theologians argue that Christians are not bound by the clear teachings of the Sermon on the Mount. Yet Jesus intended his followers to take the Sermon on the Mount very seriously as we can tell by the records left by the early Christians. There is no reason to weaken Christianity into a religion of passive faith. Through the Sermon on the Mount, Jesus called us into discipleship and challenged us to live by his direct words and instructions.

If we take the Sermon on the Mount literally, we must live by the ethics and morals Jesus himself lived by—and recommended to his followers. That is the challenge we face. With God's help, we can be transformed by living the teaching and values in the Sermon on the Mount. Even though none of us will reach perfection in this life, we are commanded to strive towards that goal. To convince you of the importance of this Christian duty, there follow passages from the Sermon on the Mount, commentaries on the excerpts, and passages from the early Christian writers who alluded to Christ's teachings.

Notes

1. Augustine as quoted in Robert Guelich, *The Sermon on the Mount* (Dallas: Word Publishing, 1982), p. 15.
2. Robert Guelich, *The Sermon on the Mount*, p. 15.
3. Robert Guelich, *The Sermon on the Mount*, p. 16.
4. Merril F. Unger, *Unger's Bible Handbook* (Chicago: Moody Press, 1966), p. 470.
5. Clarence Larkin, *Dispensational Truth* (Philadelphia: Larkin, 1918), p. 87.
6. Lewis Sperry Chafin, *Grace* (Grand Rapids: Zondervan, 1922), p. 124.
7. Robert Frost as quoted in Robert Bowman, *Sermon on the Mount* (Elgin, Illinois: Brethren Press, 1987), p. 6.

The Poor in Spirit

Blessed are the poor in spirit, for theirs is the kingdom of heaven.

—Matthew 5:3

       The Sermon on the Mount begins with eight beatitudes. The first four tell how our relationship with God is to be, while the second four tell of how our relationships with others are to be. The thoughts of the Beatitudes are intertwined, and they give us a rich picture of how the Christian life is to be lived. When we are right with God, only then can we serve others.

       The first beatitude speaks of humility before God and others. Pride, believed in the Middle Ages to be the deadliest of sins, can be overcome by following the way of this beatitude.

"Let us therefore, brethren, be of humble mind, laying aside all haughtiness and pride, and foolishness, and angry feelings; and let us act accordingly to that which is written (for the Holy Spirit saith, 'Let not the wise man glory in his wisdom, neither let the mighty man glory in his might, neither let the rich man glory in his riches; but let him glorieth glory in the Lord, in diligently seeking Him, and doing judgement and righteousness.'")

— Clement, *Epistle to the Corinthians*

"For Christ is of those who are humble-minded, and not of those who exalt themselves over His flock. Our Lord Jesus Christ, the Sceptre of the majesty of God, did not come in pomp or arrogance, although he might have done so, but in a lowly condition, as the Holy Spirit had declared regarding Him."

— Clement, *Epistle to the Corinthians*

1

"To the man who exalts and magnifies himself is attached the quick transition and the fall to low estate, as the divine word teaches."
— Clement of Alexandria, *Fragments from Antonius Melissa*

The Poor in Spirit

Why did Jesus give this beatitude as the first one?

Why must you acknowledge spiritual need to enter the kingdom of heaven?

In the middle ages, the Roman Catholic Church drew up a list of seven deadly sins. Heading the list was pride. Why do you suppose this was?

What should our attitude be towards ourself? How is this different from the emphasis of our culture?

What are ways that pride can ruin our lives and our relationships?

Might your church consider using the New Testament practice of feetwashing, taught by Jesus in John 13:1–6, illustrated in I Timothy 5:10 and recommended by Cyprian in *The Epistles of Cyprian*? What would doing this in Christian community illustrate?

Blessed Are Those Who Mourn

Blessed are those who mourn, for they will be comforted.

—Matthew 5:4

The second beatitude tells of mourning, an idea not popular today. Mourning may refer to those who have seen difficult times. It can be a deep sorrow for sin.

"But, say they, if God cares for you, why are you persecuted and put to death? Has he delivered you to this? No, we do not suppose that the Lord wishes us to be involved in calamities, but that He foretold prophetically what would happen—that we should be persecuted for His name's sake, slaughtered and impaled. So that it was not that He wishes us to be persecuted, but He intimated beforehand what we shall suffer the prediction what would take place, training us to endurance, to which He promised inheritance."

— Clement of Alexandria, *The Stromata*

"Peter, hearing this, shed tears of sympathy, and said to his friends who were present: 'If any man who is a worshipper of God had endured what this man's father has endured, immediately man would assign his religion as the cause of his calamities; but when these things happen to miserable Gentiles, they charge their misfortunes upon fate. I call them miserable because they are both vexed with errors here, and are deprived of hope; whereas, when the worshippers of God suffer these things, their patient endurance of them contributes to their cleansing of sin.'"

— *Recognitions of Clement*

"But if that evil father upon earth, deeply offended by a sinful and evil son, yet if he should see the same son afterwards reformed, and the sins of his former life put away, restored to sobriety and morality and to the discipline of innocence by the sorrow of his repentance, both rejoice and give thanks, and with the eagerness of a father's exultation, embraces the restored one, whom he had cast out; how much more does that one and true Father, good, merciful, and loving,—yea, Himself Goodness and Mercy and Love— rejoice in the repentance of His own sons! nor threatens punishment to those who are now repenting, or mourning and lamenting, but rather promises pardon and clemency. Whence the Lord in the Gospels calls those who mourn, blessed; because he who mourns calls forth mercy."

— Cyprian, *The Epistles of Cyprian*

Blessed Are Those Who Mourn

Why is this beatitude so different from the spirit of our age?

How can mourning be related to poverty of spirit?

What are injustices in our world that we ought to mourn over?

What are sins in our life that we might mourn over?

How does mourning lead to repentance?

Makarios, a figure in the early church prayed once, "O God, have mercy on me a sinner, for I have done no good before you, but deliver me from the devil. Forgive me, the sinner, the evil, the liar, the impatient, the faint-hearted and indolent, the negligent of your holy commandments, the one who has done all and every sin and transgression." He was a good man. How is his prayer different from those we offer to God?

Blessed Are the Meek

Blessed are the meek, for they will inherit the earth.

—Matthew 5:5

Meek people are humble and open to others and to God. Their lives are under control, and they have the proper behavior for various situations. We may see the meek as doormats, but in reality they have great power. God, not passions, rules the meek.

"Because He brought all things to bear on the discipline of the soul, he said, 'Blessed are the meek; for they shall inherit the earth.' And the meek are those who have quelled the battle of unbelief in the soul, the battle of wrath and lust, and the other forms that are subject to them. And He praises those meek by choice, not by necessity."

— Clement of Alexandria, *The Stromata*

"My child, be nor a murmerer, since it leads the way to blasphemy; neither self-willed or evil-minded, for out of all these blasphemies are engendered. But be meek, since the meek shall inherit the earth. Be long-suffering and pitiful and guileless and gentle and good and always trembling at the words you have heard. You shalt not exalt thyself, nor give overconfidence to your soul. Your soul shall not be joined with lofty ones, but with just and lowly ones shall it have its intercourse. Your works that befall you receive as good, knowing apart from God nothing comes to pass."

— Polycarp, *The Teaching of the Twelve Apostles*

"Be not a murmerer, remembering the punishment which those underwent who murmered against Moses. Be not self-willed, be not malicious, be not hardhearted, be not passionate, be not meanspirited; for all these things lead to blasphemy. But be meek, as were Moses and David, since the meek shall inherit the earth.'"

— *Constitutions of the Holy Apostles*

"Be humble in response to their wrath, oppose to their blasphemies your earnest prayers; while they go astray, stand you steadfast in the faith. Conquer their harsh temper by gentleness, their passion by meekness. But 'blessed are the meek'; and Moses was meek above all men; and David was exceeding meek. Wherefore Paul exhorts as follows: 'The servant of the Lord must not strive, but be gentle towards all men, apt to teach, patient in meekness, instructing those who oppose themselves.'"

— Ignatius, *Epistle to the Ephesians*

"There are three passions, or, so to speak, three furies, which excite such great perturbations in the souls of men, and compel them to offend in such a manner, as to permit them to have regard neither for their reputation nor their personal safety; these are anger, which desires vengeance; love of gain, which longs for riches; lust, which seeks for pleasure. We must above all things resist these vices: these trunks must be rooted up, that virtues may be implanted. These passions, therefore, must be kept within their boundries and directed into their right course, in which, even though they should be vehement, they cannot incur blame."

—Lactantius, *The Epitome of the Divine Institutes*

Blessed Are the Meek

What is meekness not?

Why was Moses considered to be the "meekest of all men"?

How does this statement compare with our worldly concepts of power and strength?

What causes you to lose your self-control?

What passions do you need to bring under control?

Hunger and Thirst for Righteousness

Blessed are those who hunger and thirst for righteousness, for they will be filled.

—Matthew 5:6

Many parts of the evangelical, Protestant world speak of an "instant salvation." If you pray a certain prayer, you are immediately "saved" and your eternal destiny is settled. Salvation for the early Christians was a journey of obedience and spiritual growth that happened throughout life. This beatitude refers to such a process.

"Wherefore let us give up vain and fruitless cares, and approach to the glorious and venerable rule of our holy calling. Let us attend to what is good, pleasing, and acceptable in the sight of Him who formed us. Let us look steadfastly to the blood of Christ, and see how precious that blood is to God which, having been shed for our salvation, has set the grace of repentance before the whole world."

— Clement, *First Clement*

"Take heed, beloved, lest His many kindness lead to the condemnation of us all. For thus it must be unless we walk worthy of Him, and with one mind do the things that are good and well pleasing in his sight."

— Clement, *First Clement*

"I write to all the churches, and impress on them all, that I shall willingly die for God, unless you hinder me. I beseech of you not to show an unseasonable goodness towards me. Suffer me to become food for the wild beasts, through whose instrumentality it will be granted me to attain to God. I am the wheat of God, and am grounded by the teeth of the wild beasts, that I may be found to be the pure bread of God. Rather entice the wild beasts, that they may become my tomb, and my leave nothing of my body; so that when I have fallen asleep in death, I may not be found troublesome to anyone."

— Ignatius, *Epistle to the Romans*

"What more could Christ declare unto us? How more could He stimulate the works of our righteousness and mercy, than by saying that whatever is given to the needy and poor is given to Himself, and by saying that He is aggrieved unless the needy and poor be supplied? So that he who in the Church is not moved by consideration for his brother, may yet be moved by contemplation of Christ; and he who does think of his fellow-servant in suffering and poverty, may yet think of his Lord, who abideth in that very man he is despising."

— Cyprian, *The Treatises of Cyprian*

Hunger and Thirst for Righteousness

Who do you know that seeks Christ and his kingdom above all else? What inspires you about this person?

What is a characteristic of a hungry or a thirsty person?

What are some Christian goals and standards you might set for your life?

What does this "righteousness" that is mentioned refer to?

What needs of the world might you minister to?

What things are there in your life that hinder your relationship with God and others?

What is your impression of Ignatius' saying telling of his upcoming martyrdom?

Blessed Are the Merciful

Blessed are the merciful, for they will be shown mercy.
—Matthew 5:7

The early Christians weren't involved in action to restructure society, but they had a keen interest in the poor and the broken of society. The Hebrew word for mercy, *chesedh*, means to get inside another person's thought and personality so we feel and see what they do. When we do that, we can minister and care for others.

"I have said what is due to God, I will now say what is to be given to man; although this very thing which you give to man is given to God, for man is in the image of God. But, however, the first office of justice is to be united with God, the second with man. But the former is called religion; and the second is called mercy or kindness; which virtue is peculiar to the just, and the worshippers of God, because this alone comprises the principle of common life . . . Therefore kindness is the greatest bond of human society; and he who has broken this is deemed impious."
— Lactantius, *The Epitome of the Divine Institutes*

"We who valued above all things the acquisition of wealth and possessions, now bring what we have into a common stock, and communicate to every one in need; we who hated and destroyed one another, and on account of their different tribe, now, since the coming of Christ live familiarly with them."
— Justin Martyr, *The First Apology*

"On the monthly day, if he likes, each puts in a small donation; but only if it be his pleasure, and only if he be able: for there is no compulsion; all is

9

voluntary. These gifts are, as it were, piety's deposit fund. For they are not taken thence and spent on feasts, and drinking bouts, and eating-houses, but to support and bury poor people, to supply the wants of boys and girls destitute of means and parents, and of old persons confined now to the house; such too, as have suffered shipwreck; and if there happens to be any in the mines, or banished to the islands, or shut up in prisons, for nothing but their fidelity the cause of God's church, they become the nurselings of their confessions . . . See how they love one another."

— Tertullian, *Apology*

"What more could Christ declare unto us? How more could He stimulate the works of our righteousness and mercy, than by saying that whatever is given to the needy and poor is given to Himself, and by saying that He is aggrieved unless the needy and poor be supplied? So that he who in the church is not moved by consideration for his brother, may yet be moved by contemplation of Christ; and he who does not think of his fellow-servant in suffering and poverty, may yet think of his Lord, who abideth in that very man he is despising."

— Cyprian, *The Treatises of Cyprian*

Blessed Are the Merciful

What do you do to promote unity and community among those you are in contact with?

What does your church do to promote unity and community among those you are in contact with?

How is this beatitude different from a call to restructure society?

Do you see the presence of Christ in the sick, the poor, and the outcasts?

Which groups or individuals have special needs today?

Do you show respect of those who disagree with you and your ideas?

Why must mercy go beyond a simple emotional feeling?

The Pure in Heart

Blessed are the pure in heart, for they will see God.

—Matthew 5:8

The Jewish temple rituals of Jesus' day used only pure gold, pure olive oil, and pure incense. Like these items, the followers of Jesus are to be pure. The early Christian writers stressed that pure lives came from a right relationship with God and pure thinking.

"Wherefore it is said, 'Blessed are the pure in heart, for they shall see God.' But as the strength of our will is not sufficient to procure the perfectly pure heart, and as we need that God should create it, he therefore who prays as he ought, offers this petition to God, 'Create in me a clean heart, O God.'"

— Origen, *Origen Against Celsus*

"And since there are two paths of reaching the perfection of salvation, works and knowledge, He called the 'pure in heart blessed, for they shall see God.' And if we really look to the truth of the matter, knowledge is the purification of the lead faculty of the soul, and is a good activity."

— Clement of Alexandria, *The Stromata*

The Pure in Heart

What does it mean to be pure in heart?

In what ways do you know God's presence in your life?

11

How many of your thoughts concentrate on God and God's kingdom?

What are your motives when you do good things for others?

What are the differences between your actions in public and private?

What does your prayer life look life?

Blessed Are the Peacemakers

Blessed are the peacemakers, for they will be called sons of God.

—Matthew 5:9

As noted earlier, the beatitudes build on one another. Inner purity leads to outward peace and joy. We know peace through the indwelling Christ, as noted in Romans 5:1 and Colossians 1:19.

"'Blessed, then, are the peacemakers,' who have subdued and tamed the law which wars against the disposition of the mind, the menaces of anger, and the baits of lust, and the other passions which war against the reason; who, having lived in the knowledge of both good works and true reason, shall be reinstated in adoption, which is dearer."

— Clement of Alexandria, *The Stromata*

"As regards the rule of peace, which is so pleasing to God, who in the world that is prone to impatience will even once forgive his brother, I will not say 'seven times,' or 'seventy-seven times.'"

— Tertullian, *Of Patience*

"Choose therefore rather to suffer harm, and to endeavour after those things that make for peace, not only among the brethren, but also among the unbelievers. For by suffering loss in the affairs of this life, you will be sure not to suffer in the concerns of piety, and will live religiously, and according to the command of Christ . . . For so would our Lord have us truly to be His disciples, and never to have anything against anybody; as for instance, anger without measure, passion without mercy, covetousness with justice, hatred without reconciliation. Draw by your instruction those who are angry to friendship, and those who are at variance to agreement. For the Lord says: 'Blessed are the peacemakers, for they shall be called the children of God.'"

—*Constitutions of the Holy Apostles*

Blessed Are the Peacemakers

Where must peace begin according to our quote from Clement of Alexandria?

What is the connection between peace and justice regarding the church's witness to the structures of society?

How is your value system different from that of the world?

How would this beatitude have sounded to the Jews who wanted to overthrow the Roman empire?

Who could you approach that has a broken relationship with you?

What can you do to promote unity and cooperation in your church?

What are things that Satan can do to disturb our peace, both personally and professionally?

Blessed Are the Persecuted

Blessed are those who are persecuted because of righteousness, for theirs is the kingdom of heaven. Blessed are you when people insult you, persecute you and falsely say all kinds of evil against you because of me. Rejoice and be glad, because great is your reward in heaven, for in the same way they persecuted the prophets who were before you.

—Matthew 5:10–12

A well-known television evangelist has a song, "Something good is going to happen to you, this very day, this very day. Something good is going to happen to you, Jesus of Nazareth is passing your way." The Christians in the first century of the church saw terrible things happen to them on many occasions. In our own century, the same thing has held true with Christians in Communist and Muslim lands. Tertullian made the bold statement, "The blood of the martyrs is the seed of the church."

"First, they seized an old man named Mestras, and ordered him to utter blasphemous words; when he refused, they beat him with cudgels, drove pointed reeds into his face and eyes, took him to the suburbs, and stoned him to death. Next, they took a female convert named Quinta to the idol's temple and tried to make her worship. When she turned her back in disgust they tied her feet and dragged her right through the city over the rough paved road, bumping her on the great stones and beating her as they went, till they arrived at the same place, where they stoned her to death. Then they all ran in a body to the houses of the Christians, charged in by groups they knew as neighbors, raised, plundered, and looted. The more valuable of their possessions they purloined; the cheaper wooden things they threw about, or they made a bonfire of them in the streets, making the city look as if it had been captured by enemies. The Christians retired and gradually withdrew; like those to whom Paul paid tribute, they took with cheerfulness the plundering of their belongings. I do not know of anyone, except possibly one man who fell into their clutches, who up to now has denied the Lord.

Next, they seized the wonderful old lady Apollania, battered her till they knocked out all her teeth, built a pyre in front of the city, and threatened to burn her alive unless she repeated after them their heathen incantations. She asked for a breathing-space, and when they released her, jumped without hesitation into the fire and was burnt to ashes. Serapion they arrested in his own house. They racked him with horrible torture and broke all his limbs, then threw him down head first from the upper floor. No road, no highway, no alley was open to us, either by night or by day; always and everywhere, everybody was shouting that anyone who did not join in their blasphemous chants must at once be dragged away and burnt."

— Eusebius, *The History of the Church*

"The Roman Senate, successive emporers, the army, the people, the very kindred of the faithful, all conspired for the destruction of the Christians."

— Origen, *Origen Against Celsus*

"But let us pass from ancient examples to those who contend for the faith in our own time. It was due to jealousy and envy that the greatest and most righteous pillars (of the Church) were persecuted and contended to the death. Let us set before our eyes the good apostles. There was Peter, who because of unrighteous jealousy endured not one or two but many hardships, and having borne his witness, went to the place of glory he deserved. Because of jealousy and strife, Paul showed how to win the prize of patient endurance. Seven times he was in bonds, he was banished, he was stoned, he became a messenger of the gospel in both east and west, and earned well-merited fame for his faith; for he taught righteousness to the whole world, having traveled to the limits of the west; and when he had borne his witness before the rulers, he departed from the world an outstanding example of patient endurance."

— Clement, *Epistle to the Corinthians*

"Let us therefore renounce our parents, and kinsmen, and friends, and wife, and children, and possessions, and all the enjoyments of life, when any of these things become an impediment to piety. For we ought to pray that we may not enter into temptation; but if we be called by martyrdom, with constancy to confess His precious name, and if on account of this be punished, let us rejoice, as hastening on to immortality. When we are persecuted, let us not think it strange; let us not love the present world, nor the praises which come from men, nor the glory and honor of the rulers."

— *Constitutions of the Holy Apostles*

Blessed Are the Persecuted

What are some reasons for us to rejoice when persecuted for Christ's sake?

How do our scripture and quotes fit with a well-known television evangelist's statement, "Something good is going to happen to you today?"

What does Tertullian's statement, "The blood of the martyrs is the seed of Christianity," mean?

How can you become more aware of Christians around the world who today suffer and die for their faith?

Why has the church in our country remained relatively silent about Christian martyrdom in our own century? It is estimated, for example, that twenty million Christians were put to death during the years of communism in the Soviet Union.

How do you see persecution of Christians in our own time and culture?

What are areas in which you are willing to go against the norms of society for your Christian witness?

How can our witnessing to others be more important about the cost of following Jesus Christ in obedience and discipleship?

Salt and Light

You are the salt of the earth. But if the salt loses its saltiness, how can it be made salty again? It is no longer good for anything, except to be thrown out and trampled by men.

You are the light of the world. A city on a hill cannot be hidden. Neither do people light a lamp and put it under a bowl. Instead they put it on its stand, and it gives light to everyone in the house. In the same way, let your light so shine before men, that they may see your good deeds and praise your Father in heaven.

—Matthew 5:13–16

These verses tell of the influence of the early Christians. Salt was valuable in New Testament times, being pure and preserving things. Light transformed darkness, leading people in the correct way of living.

Early Christianity was known for rapid growth and evangelism. Faith sharing took place in informal settings, the home and the workplace. It was risky to share faith, for a spouse might turn a mate in to the authorities. Holy living helped win many to Christ.

"Since the Lord warns us, saying, 'Ye are the salt of the earth,' and since He bids us to be simple and harmless, and yet with our simplicity to be prudent, what else, beloved brethren, befits us, than to use foresight and watching with an anxious heart."

— Cyprian, *The Treatises of Cyprian*

"All of the faithful, then, are good and godlike, and worthy of the name by which they are encircled as with a diadem. They are, besides, some, like and elect, and so much more or less distinguished by drawing themselves, like ships to the strand, out of the surge of the world and bringing themselves to be holy, and ashamed if one calls them so; hiding in the depth of their mind the ineffable mysteries, and disdaining to let their nobleness to be seen in the world; whom the Word calls 'the light of the world and in Him there is no darkness at all.'"

> — Origen, *Origen Against Celsus*

"Our earnest desire then is both to see for ourselves, and to be leaders of the blind, to bring them to the Word of God, that He may take away from their minds the blindness of ignorance. And if our actions are worthy of Him who taught His disciples, 'You are the light of the world,' and of the Word who says, 'The light shineth in the darkness,' then we shall be light to those in darkness; we shall give wisdom to those who are without it, and we shall instruct the ignorant."

> — Origen, *Origen Against Celsus*

"Let all things be done with modesty, courteousness, affability and uprighteousness, so that the name of our God and our Lord Jesus Christ may be glorified among all."

> — Theonas, *The Epistle of Theonas*

"We see, indeed, in private houses workers in wool and leather, and fullers, and persons of rustic character, not venturing to utter a word in the presence of their elders and wiser masters; but they get hold of the children privately, and certain women as ignorant as themselves, they pour forth wonderful statements."

> — Origen, *Origen Against Celsus*

"But as to a spirit of contention, be sure to curb it as to all men, but principally to thine husband; lest, if he be an unbeliever or an heathen, he may have an occasion of scandal or by blaspheming God, and thou be partaker of a woe from God . . . You wives, therefore, demonstrate your piety by your modesty and your meekness to all without the Church, whether they be women or men, in order to their conversion and improvement in the faith."

> — *Constitutions of the Holy Apostles*

"See, then, that they be instructed by your works, if in no other way. Be ye meek in response to their wrath, humble in opposition to their boasting: to their blasphemies return your prayers; in constraint to their error, be ye steadfast in their faith; and for their cruelty, manifest your gentleness."

> — Ignatius, *Epistle to the Ephesians*

"Therefore, brethren, let us now at last repent and take sober thought of what is good; for we are full of much folly and evil. We must remove our former sins from ourselves and by wholehearted repentance be saved. Let us not seek to please men, nor yet please ourselves only; yet we must commend ourselves to outsiders in righteousness, lest the name be blasphemed on account of us."

— Clement, *II Clement*

Salt and Light

How might a Christian loose his "saltiness"?

What were the functions of salt in the ancient world, and what do they tell us about the Christian?

How might you put a bowl over the light of Christ that lives in you?

What is your Christian testimony, and have you shared it with others?

Whom have you involved in your church during the last few years?

What about your church would you like to see changed so that those on the outside would find it more attractive?

Have there been times when you would rather not have been identified as a Christian?

Do Not Think That I Have Come to Abolish the Law or the Prophets

Do not think that I have come to abolish the Law or the Prophets: I have not come to abolish them but to fulfill them. I tell you the truth, until heaven and earth disappear, not the smallest letter, not the least stroke of a pen, will by any means disappear from the Law until everything is accomplished. Anyone who breaks one of the least of these commands and teachers others to do the same will be called least in the kingdom of heaven, but whoever practices and teaches these commands will be called great in the kingdom of heaven. For I tell you that unless your righteousness surpasses that of the Pharisees and the teachers of the Law, you will certainly now enter the kingdom of heaven.

—Matthew 5:17–20

In some evangelical Christian circles, it is stressed that having Jesus Christ as one's savior does not necessitate having Christ as Lord. These groups stress free salvation as gift, with nothing expected in return. This may lead to "antionomianism," the idea that we are freed from the requirements of the law.

These verses stress, however, that Jesus calls for a new righteousness from his followers. One must go beyond Old Testament legalism to find the freeing law of Christian love. Several examples of how this can happen are found in the rest of Matthew 5. Our study of the early Christian writers can keep this in focus.

☩

"For He exhorted His disciples to surpass the pharisaic way of living, with the warning that if they did not they might be sure they could not be saved; and these words are recorded in the memoirs: 'Unless your righteousness exceed that of the Scribes and the Pharisees, ye shall not enter into the kingdom of heaven.'"

— Justin Martyr, *Dialogue with Trypho*

21

"Now you ought to know, that although the Lord has delivered you from the additional bonds, and has brought you out of them to your refreshment, and does not permit you to sacrifice irrational creatures for your sin-offerings, and purifications, and scapegoats, and continued washings and sprinklings, yet He nowhere freed you from these oblations which you owe the priests, nor from doing good to the poor. For the Lord says to you in the Gospel: 'Unless your righteousness abound more than that of the scribes and the Pharisees, ye shall by no means enter into the kingdom of heaven.' Now herein will your righteousness exceed theirs, if you take care of the priests, the orphans, the widows, for it is written: 'He hath scattered abroad; he hath given to the poor; his righteousness remaineth forever.'"

— Constitutions of the Holy Apostles

"We ought to remember by what name Christ calls His people, by what title He names His flock. He calls them sheep, that their Christian innocence may be like that of sheep; He calls them lambs, that their simplicity of mind may imitate the simple nature of lambs. Why does the wolf lurk under the garb of the sheep? To put on the name of Christ, and not go in the way of Christ is but a mockery of the divine name, but a desertion of the way of salvation; since He Himself teaches and says that he who shall come unto life who keeps His commandments, and he is wise who hears and does his words; that he, moreover, is called the greatest doctor in the kingdom of heaven who thus does and teaches."

— Cyprian, The Treatises of Cyprian

The Law or the Prophets

List some of the laws of our society. Why are these laws necessary?

What does Jesus' words on the law and the prophets refer to?

How can your righteousness exceed that of the Scribes and the Pharisees?

Looking at the remainder of Matthew 5, what are the inner attitudes that Jesus wants changed?

How do you apply Jesus' wisdom to these areas of your life?

What should a Christian living a holy life be like?

Why must Christ be both our Savior and our Lord?

Do Not Be Angry

You have heard that it was said to people of long ago, 'Do not murder, and anyone who murders will be subject to judgment.' But I tell you that anyone who is angry with his brother will be subject to judgment. Again, anyone who says to his brother, 'Raca,' is answerable to the Sanhedrin. But anyone who says, 'You fool!' will be in danger of the fire of hell.

Therefore, if you are offering your gift at the altar and there remember that your brother has something against you, leave your gift there in front of the altar. First go and be reconciled to your brother; then come and offer your gift.

Settle matters quickly with your adversary who is taking you to court. Do it while you are still with him on the way, or he may hand you over to the judge, and the judge may hand you over to the officer, and you may be thrown into prison. I tell you the truth, you will not get out until you have paid the last penny.

—Matthew 5:21–26

While the Old Testament law forbids murder, the new law that Jesus brought forbids murder in our thought life. Anger is an emotion that happens to all of us. Jesus himself sometimes became angry, as in Mark 3:5.

The problem Jesus speaks of us is escalating anger, anger that leads to violence or to long-standing grudges. Anger hurts our inner spiritual state if unresolved, as well as others. Problems with others are to be openly confronted and then resolved, if at all possible. God's forgiving grace gives us an example of what Jesus expects us to do.

"'Be angry and sin not,' that is, be soon reconciled, lest your wrath continue so long that it turns into a settled hatred, and work sin."

— *Constitutions of the Holy Apostles*

"Now the gift to God is everyone's prayer and thanksgiving. If, therefore, you have anything against your brother, or if he has anything against you, neither will your prayers be heard, nor will your thanksgiving be accepted, by reason of that hidden anger. But it is your duty, brethren, to pray continuously."

— Constitutions of the Holy Apostles

"Nay, if you have remitted to your brother four hundred and ninety times forgiveness, continue still to multiply your gentleness more, to do good for thy sake. Although he does not do so yet, however, do endeavour to forgive your brothers for God's sake, 'that you may be the son of your Father which is in heaven,' and when you pray, you may be heard as a friend of God."

— Constitutions of the Holy Apostles

"It is also a duty to forgive each others trespasses—not the duty of those that judge, but of those who have quarrels ... Our Lord would have us to be truly His disciples, and never to have anything against anybody; as, for instance, anger without measure, passion without mercy, covetousness with justice, hatred without reconciliation."

— Constitutions of the Holy Apostles

"But every Lord's day, do gather yourselves together, and break bread, and give thanksgiving after having confessed your transgressions, that your sacrifices be pure. But let no one that is at variance with his fellows come together with you, until they be reconciled, that your sacrifice may not be profaned."

— Polycarp, The Teaching of the Twelve Apostles

"For men of old wanted to require 'eye for eye, and tooth for tooth,' and to repay with usury, 'evil with evil'; for, as yet, patience was not on earth, because faith was not either. Of course, meantime, impatience was not on earth, because faith was not either. Of course, meantime, impatience used to enjoy the opportunities the law gave. That was easy, while the Lord and Master of patience was absent. But after he was present, and has united the grace of faith with patience, now it is no longer to assail even word against word, nor to say 'feel,' even, without 'danger of the judgement.' Anger has been prohibited, our spirits retained, the petulance of the hand checked, and the poison of the tongue extracted."

—Cyprian, Of Patience

Do Not Be Angry

What do the following verses teach about anger?
Psalm 37:8
Proverbs 16:32
Proverbs 19:11
Ecclesiastes 7:9
James 1:19

What actions and attitudes are included in Jesus' statement, "Do not murder?"

What is the difference between judgement and discernment?

Who should take the initiative in relationships when others are strained?

What can anger and broken relationships do to us over an extended period of time?

What do you think about the statement, "The way we treat others is the way we treat God?"

The New Law Regarding Marriage

You have heard it was said, 'Do not commit adultery.' But I tell you that anyone who looks at a woman lustfully has already committed adultery with her in his heart. If your right eye causes you to sin, gouge it out and throw it away. It is better for you to lose one part of your body than for your whole body to be thrown into hell. And if your right hand causes you to sin, cut it off and throw it away. It is better for you to lose one part of your body than for your whole body to go to hell.

It has been said, 'Anyone who divorces his wife must give her a certificate of divorce.' But I tell you that anyone who divorces his wife, except for marital unfaithfulness, causes her to commit adultery, and anyone who marries a woman so divorced commits adultery.

—Matthew 5:27–32

Human sexuality is a good gift from God when used in the proper channels. Lust and promiscuity are not to be indulged in. Impure thinking leads to sinful and shameful acts.

"For as our bodies are members of Christ, and we are each a temple of God, whosoever violates the temple of God by adultery, violates God; and he who, in committing sins, does the will of the devil, serves demons and idols. For evil deeds do not come from the Holy Spirit, but from the prompting of the adversary, and lusts, born of unclean spirit, constrain men to act against God and obey the devil."

— Cyprian, *The Epistles of Cyprian*

"But adultery and fornication are against the law, the one is concerned with impiety, the other injustice, and in a word, both are great sins. Those of the second sort—the adulterers—are unjust by corrupting others' marriages, and dividing in two what God has made one, rendering children suspected, and exposing the true husband to the snares of others."

— *Constitutions of the Holy Apostles*

27

"So, too, whoever enjoys any other than nuptial intercourse, in whatever place, and in the person of whatever woman, makes himself guilty of adultery and fornication. Frenzies of passions—impious both toward the bodies and toward the sexes—beyond all the laws of nature, we banish not only from the threshold, but from all the shelter of the Church, since they are not sins, but monstrosities."

— Tertullian, *On Modesty*

"And concerning chastity, the holy word teaches us not only to sin in act, but not even in thought, not even in the heart of evil, nor look upon another man's wife with our eyes to lust after her."

— Theophilus, *To Autolycus*

"So that all, who by human law, are twice married, are in the eye of our Master sinners, and those who look upon a woman to lust after her. For not only he who commits adultery is rejected by Him, but also he who desires to commit adultery; since not only our works, but also our thoughts, are open to God."

— Justin Martyr, *The First Apology*

The New Law Regarding Marriage

What is sin according to the definition mentioned here?

How is thinking related to action?

How can our thought process be transformed?

How can we witness to society and to others the values of integrity and fidelity in our lives?

What habits do you have that you find very hard to change?

The New Law About Honesty

Again, you have heard that it was said to the people long ago, 'Do not break your oath, but keep the oaths you have made to the Lord.' But I tell you, Do not swear at all: either by heaven, for it is God's footstool; or my Jerusalem, for it is the city of the Great King. And do not swear by your head, for you cannot make even one hair white or black. Simply let your 'Yes' be 'Yes,' and your 'No,' 'No': anything beyond this comes from the evil one.

—Matthew 5:33–37

Jesus called for people to be honest. While the Old Testament Jews took oaths, God's people under the new covenant were forbidden to.

✟

"Of false swearing I am silent, since even swearing is not lawful."
— Tertullian, *On Idolatry*

"Wherefore it is the duty of a man of God, as he is a Christian, not to swear by the sun, or by the moon, or by the stars; nor by the heaven, nor by the earth, nor by any of the elements, whether small or great. For if our Master charged us not to swear by the true God, that our word might be firmer than an oath, for this custom is a piece of Judaic corruption, and on that account was forbidden."
— *Constitutions of the Holy Apostles*

The New Law About Honesty

How can we have honesty and integrity in our lives?

Does this mean that we should never take an oath in a court of law? (Some Anabaptists, including Quakers, do not.)

How would simple truthfulness and integrity help business, the community, marriage, the church, and government?

What would be an area in your life that you might be more honest?

Love Your Enemies

You have heard that it was said, 'An eye for an eye and a tooth for a tooth.' But I say to you, Do not resist one who is evil. But if any one strikes you on the right cheek, turn to him the other also; and if any one would sue you and take your cloak, let him have your cloack as well; and if any one forces you to go one mile, go with him two miles. Give to him who begs from you, and do not refuse him who would borrow from you.

You have heard that it was said, 'You shall love your neighbor and hate your enemy.' But I say to you, Love your enemies and pray for those who persecute you, so that you may be sons of your Father who is in heaven; for he makes his sun rise on the evil and on the good, and sends rail on the just and on the unjust. For if you love those who love you, what reward have you? Do not even the tax collectors do the same? And if you salute only your brethren, what more are you doing than others? Do not even the Gentiles do the same? You, therefore, must be perfect, as your heavenly Father is perfect.

—Matthew 5:38–48

The early Christians took these words literally. There is no record of any Christian serving in the military until the reign of Marcus Aurelius (161 to 180 A.D.) Much of the power of early Christianity came in the love shared with all.

"We who formerly used to murder one another do not only refrain from making war upon our enemies, but also, that we may not lie nor deceive our examiners, willingly die confessing Christ."

— Justin Martyr, *The First Apology*

"Pray also for kings, and potentates, and princes, and for those that persecute you and hate you, and for the enemies of the cross, that your fruit may be manifest to all, and that ye might be perfect in Him."

— Polycarp, *The Epistle of Polycarp*

"In the last section, decision may seem to have given likewise concerning military service, which is between dignity and power. But now inquiry is made about this point, whether a believer may turn himself unto military service, and whether the military may be admitted into the faith, even the rank and file, or each inferior grace, to whom there is no necessity, for taking part in sacrifices or capital punishments. There is no agreement between the divine and the human standard, the standard of Christ and the standard of the devil, the camp of light and the camp of darkness. One soul cannot be two masters—God and Caesar . . . But how will a Christian man war, nay, how will he serve even in peace, without a sword, which the Lord has taken away? . . . The Lord, in disarming Peter, unbelted every soldier."

— Tertullian, *On Idolatry*

"To begin with the real ground of the military crown, I think we must first inquire whether warfare is proper at all for Christians . . . Shall it be lawful to make an occupation of the sword, when the Lord proclaims that he who uses the sword shall perish by the sword? And shall the son of peace take part in battle when it does not become him even to sue at law? And shall he apply the chain and the prison, and the torture, and the punishment, who is not the avenger even of his wrong? Shall he keep guard over the temples which he has renounced? Shall he take a meal where the apostle has forbidden him? . . . Then how many other offences there are involved in the performance of camp offices, which we must hold to involve a transgression of God's law, you may see by a slight survey. The very carrying of the name over the camp of light to the camp of darkness is a violation of it."

— Tertullian, *De Corona*

"How you inflict gross cruelties on Christians, partly because it is your own inclination and partly in obedience to the laws! How often, too, the hostile mob, paying no regard to you, takes the law into its own hand, and assails us with stones and flames. With the very frenzy of the Bacchanals, they do not even spare the Christian dead, but tear them into pieces, rendering them assunder. Yet, banded together as we are, ever so ready to sacrifice our lives, what single case of revenge for injury are you able to point to, though, if it were right among us to repay evil for evil, a single night with a torch or two would achieve an ample vengence?"

— Tertullian, *Apology*

"Consider the roads blocked by robbers, the seas beset by pirates, wars scattered over all the earth with the bloody horror of the camps. The whole

world is set with a mutual blood; and murder, which is in the case of an individual is considered a crime, is called a virtue when it is committed wholesale. Impunity is claimed for the wicked deeds, not on the plea that they are guiltless, but because the cruelty is perpetrated on a grand scale."
— Cyprian, *The Epistles of Cyprian*

"There are two ways, one of life and one of death; but a great difference between the two ways. The way of life, then, is this: First, thou shalt love God who made thee; second, thy neighbor as thyself; and all things whatsoever thou wouldst not occur to thee, thou also to another do not do. And of these sayings the teaching is this: Bless them that curse you, and pray for your enemies, and fast for them that persecute you, for what thanks is there, if ye love them that love you? Do not also the Gentiles do the same ... If one give thee a blow upon thy right cheek, turn to him the other also; and thou shalt be perfect."
— Polycarp, *The Teaching of the Twelve Apostles*

Love Your Enemies

Who are your enemies? How do you show love to them?

What might you do to show love to your enemies that you aren't doing now?

How do you involve your enemies in your prayer life?

How did Jesus treat his enemies at the time of his death (read Matthew 26:47–68, 1 Peter 2:23, and Matthew 23:26–34)?

How should the church today respond to issues of war and peace?

What is your understanding of verse forty-eight, "You, therefore, must be perfect, as your heavenly Father is perfect."

Motives and Giving

Beware of practicing your piety before men in order to be seen by them; for then you will have no reward from your Father who is in heaven. Thus, when you give alms, sound no trumpet before you, as the hypocrites do in the synagogues and in the streets, that they may be praised by men. Truly I say to you, they have their reward. But when you give alms, do not let your left hand know what your right hand is doing, so that your alms may be in secret; and your Father who sees in secret will reward you.

—Matthew 6:1–4

The Jewish, Islam, and Christian faith have traditionally had three great pillars of devotion. Giving, prayer, and fasting can bring people close to God, or they can bring attention to ourselves. Matthew 6:1–16 tells of pure motives for giving, prayer, and fasting. The first section, Matthew 6:1–4, tells of giving.

☩

"To him the flesh is dead; but he himself lives alone, having consecrated the sepulchre into a holy temple to the Lord, having turned towards God the old sinful soul. Such a one is no longer continent, but has reached a state of passionless, waiting to put on the divine image. 'If thou doest alms,' it is said, 'let no one know it; and if thou fastest anoint thyself, that God alone may know,' and not a single human being. Not even he himself who shows mercy ought to know that he does show mercy; for in this way he will be sometimes merciful, sometimes not. And when he shall do good by habit, he will imitate the nature of good, and his disposition will be his nature and his practice."

— Clement of Alexandria, *The Stromata*

"An illustrious and divine thing, dearest brethren, is the saving labour of charity, a great comfort of believers, a wholesome guard of our security, a protection of hope, a safeguard of faith, a remedy of sin, a thing placed in the power of the doer, a thing both great and easy, a crown of peace without the risk of persecution; the true and greatest gift of God, needful for the weak, glorious for the strong, assisted by which the Christian accomplishes spiritual grace.

— Cyprian, *The Treatises of Cyprian*

"All the first-fruits of the winepress, the threshing floor, the oxen, and the sheep, shalt thou give to the priests, that thy storehouses and garners and the products of thy land be blessed, and thou mayest be strengthened with corn and wine and oil, and the herds thy cattle and flocks of thy sheep may be increased. Thou shalt give the tenth of thy increase to the orphan, to the widow, and to the poor, and to the stranger. All the first-fruits of thy hot bread, or thy barrels of wine, or oil, or honey, or nuts, or grapes, of the first-fruits of other things, shalt thou give to the priests; but those of silver, and of garments, and of all sort of possessions, to the orphans and the widow."

— *Constitutions of the Holy Apostles*

"Notice that he has not told you to wait until someone asks or begs you to share your wealth. No. You yourself must look for those worthy disciples of the Savior whom you can aid. As the apostle has most excellently put it, 'the Lord loves a cheerful giver.' (II Corinthians 9:7) The cheerful giver delights in giving. He does it without murmuring, disputing, or showing regret. This is giving that is pure. Even more blessed is what the Lord said in another place: 'Give to everyone who asks you.' (Luke 6:30) This shows how delighted God is when we give. And this saying is above all divinity: not wanting to be asked, but finding out for ourselves who deserves to receive kindness."

— Clement of Alexandria, *Who Is The Rich Man That Shall Be Saved*

"What a rich reward God promises us for our generous giving: an eternal dwelling place. What an excellent trade! What divine merchandise! We can purchase immortality with money. By giving up the perishing things of this world, we can receive an eternal mansion in heaven. Sail to this market, if you are wise, rich man."

— Clement of Alexandria,*Who Is The Rich Man That Shall Be Saved*

"Prayers must be holy, sent without crime. The 'altar' tells, if you do offer gifts, must first be reconciled with peace with your brother; thus at length his prayers can flame unto the stars."

— Tertullian, *Appendix*

Motives and Giving

Who is a religious or pious person you respect, and why?

What does it mean to have God as our Father?

Why should our giving be in secret?

What are the rewards of faithful stewardship?

How might you restructure your life to make more resources available to others?

If the Old Testament expected tithing, what should we as Christians give?

The Lord's Prayer

But when you pray, do not be like the hypocrites, for they love to pray standing in the synogogues and on the street corners to be seen by men. I tell you the truth, they have received their reward in full. When you pray, go into your room, close the door and pray to your Father, who is unseen. Then your Father, who sees what is done in secret, will reward you. And when you pray, do not keep on babbling like pagans, for they think they will be heard because of their many words. Do not be like them, for your Father knows what you need before you ask him.

This is how you should pray: 'Our Father in heaven, hallowed be your name, your kingdom come, your will be done on earth as it is in heaven. Give us today our daily bread. Forgive our debts, as we also have forgiven our debtors. And lead us not into temptation, but deliver us from the evil one.'

For if you forgive men when they sin against you, your heavenly Father will also forgive you. But if you do not forgive men their sins, your Father will not forgive your sins.

—Matthew 6:5–15

The second pillar of devotion for early Christianity was prayer. Jesus tells in our text of praying in secret, then he gives a model prayer, the Lord's Prayer.

The Jewish prayer life that Jesus addressed was one that had become formal and sterile. The Jews had mandatory prayer each morning and evening, as well as a set of eighteen prayers that had to be recited three times each day.

Matthew 6:5–8 deals with prayer being real and not ritualistic. Following this, Jesus gives a perfect prayer that we know as the Lord's Prayer. All three early Christian liturgies in the Ante-Nicene Fathers use the Lord's Prayer as a prescribed element of worship. It was also used in private devotion.

"But we more commend our prayers to God when we pray with modesty and humility, with not even our hands too loftily elevated, but elevated temperately and becomingly; and not even our countenance over-boldly uplifted . . . The sounds of our voice, likewise, should be subdued; else, if we are to be heard for our noise, how large windpipes we should need! But God is the hearer not of the voice, but of the heart, just He is its inspector . . . What superior advantage will they who pray too loudly gain, except that they annoy their neighbours?"

— Tertullian, *On Prayer*

"And so prayer knows nothing save how to recall the souls of the departed from the very path of death, to transform the weak, to restore the sick, to purge the possessed, to open prison-bars, to loose the bonds of the innocent. Likewise it washes away all faults, repels temptations, extinguishes persecutions, consoles the faint-hearted, cheers the high-spirited, escorts travellers, appeases waves, makes robbers stand aghast, nourishes the poor, governs the rich, upraises the fallen, arrests the falling, confirms the standing. Prayer is the wall of faith: her arms and missiles against the foe who keeps watch over us on all sides. And we, we never walk unarmed. Under the arms of prayer guard we the standard of our general; await we in prayer the angel's trump."

— Tertullian, *On Prayer*

"But what matters of deep moment are contained in the Lord's prayer! How many and how great, briefly collected in words, but spiritually abundant in virtue! So there is absolutely nothing passed over that is not comprehended in these our prayers and petitions, as in a compendium of heavenly doctrine."

— Cyprian, *The Treatises of Cyprian*

"Our father who art in heaven, hallowed be your name," verse nine commentary:
"But how great is the Lord's indulgence! How great His condescension and plenteousness of goodness towards us, seeing that He has wished us to pray in the sight of God in such a way as to call God Father, and to call ourselves sons of God, even as Christ is the Son of God, — a name which none of us would dare to venture on in prayer, unless He Himself had allowed thus to pray! We ought then, beloved brethren, to remember and to know, that when we call God Father, we ought to act as God's children; so that in the measure in which we find pleasure in considering God as a Father, He might also be able to find pleasure in us.'"

— Cyprian, *The Treatises of Cyprian*

"The name of 'God the Father' had been published to none. Even Moses, who had interrogated Him on that very point, had heard a different name. To us it has been revealed in the Son, for the Son is now the Father's new name."
— Tertullian, *On Prayer*

"When we pray, 'Hallowed be Thy name,' we pray that it be hallowed in us who are in Him, as well in all others for whom the grace of God is still waiting; that we may obey this precept, too, in 'praying for all,' even for our personal enemies."
— Tertullian, *On Prayer*

"Your kingdom come, your will be done on earth as it is in heaven," verse ten commentary:
"For since He is Himself the Resurrection, since in Him we rise again, so also the kingdom of God may be understood to be himself, since in Him we shall all reign. But we do well in seeking the kingdom of God, that is, the heavenly kingdom, because there is also an earthly kingdom."
— Cyprian, *The Treatises of Cyprian*

"'Thy kingdom come' has also reference to that whereto 'Thy will be done' refers—in us, that is. For when does God not reign in whose hand is the heart of all kings. But whatever we wish for ourselves we ask from Him, and to Him we attribute from Him what we expect."
— Tertullian, *On Prayer*

"Give us this day our daily bread," verse eleven commentary:
"But how gracefully has the Divine Wisdom arranged the order of the prayer; so that things heavenly—that is, after the 'Name' of God, the 'Will' of God, and the 'Kingdom' of God—it should give earthly necessities also room for a petition!"
— Tertullian, *On Prayer*

"And this may be understood both spiritually and literally, because either way of understanding is rich in divine usefulness to our salvation. For Christ is the bread of life; and this bread does not belong to all men, but it is ours."
— Cyprian, *The Treatises of Cyprian*

"It may also be thus understood that we who have renounced the world, and have cast away its riches and pomps in the faith of spiritual grace, should only ask for ourselves food and support, since the Lord instructs us, and says, 'Whosoever forsaketh not all that he hath, cannot be my disciple.' But he who has begun to be Christ's disciple, renouncing all things, according to the words of his Master, ought to ask for his daily food, and not to extend the desires of his petition to a long period, as the

Lord again prescribes and says, 'Take no thought for the morrow itself shall take thought for itself. Sufficient for the day is the evil thereof.'"

— Cyprian, *The Treatises of Cyprian*

"Forgive us our debts, as we also have forgiven our debtors. And lead us not into temptation, but deliver us from the evil one," verse twelve and thirteen commentary:

"And how necessarily, how providently and salutarily, are we admonished that we are sinners, since we are compelled to entreat for our sins, and while pardon is asked for from God, the soul recalls its own consciousness of sin! Lest any one should flatter himself that he is innocent, and by exalting himself should more deeply perish, he is instructed and taught that he sins daily, that he is bidden to entreat daily for sins."

— Cyprian, *The Treatises of Cyprian*

The Lord's Prayer

How does this passage of the Lord's Prayer speak to your own prayer experience?

The early Christians had set times for daily private prayer. The *Didache* suggested that the Lord's Prayer be prayed three times a day. Tertullian referred to prayer at 9 a.m., noon, 3 p.m., as well as in the evening and at bedtime. Prayer was also given at meals. How might we make set times of prayer part of our day?

Clement of Alexandria wrote that a Christian "pray throughout his whole life." How can we do that?

What does it mean to hallow God's name?

What does it mean to have God's kingdom come?

How can we discover God's will in our life?

What is our daily bread?

How did Jesus make forgiveness conditional?

How do we seek deliverance from Satan?

When You Fast

When you fast, do not look somber as the hypocrites do, for they disfigure their faces to show men they are fasting. I tell you the truth, they have received their reward in full. But when you fast, put oil on your head and wash your face, so that it will not be obvious to men that you are fasting, but only to your Father, who is unseen; and your Father, who sees what is done in secret, will reward you.

—Matthew 6:16–18

How does Jesus start this section of the Sermon on the Mount? It is not with "if you fast," but rather "when you fast." Jesus expected that his followers would fast from time to time. True fasting is done in secret, and it gives us spiritual power and insight. Jesus, in Mark 9:29, explains to the disciples of his effective prayer for an epileptic child, "This kind cannot be driven out by anything but prayer and fasting."

The early Christians fasted on Wednesday and Friday. It also happened at baptism, when decisions had to be made, and on other occasions.

"Fasting, according to the significance of the word, is abstinence from food. Now food makes us neither more righteous nor less. But mystically it shows that, as life is maintained in individuals by sustenance, and want of sustenance is the token of death; so also we ought to fast from worldly things, that we may die to the world, and after that, by partaking of divine sustenance, life to God. Especially does fasting empty the soul of matter, and make it, along with the body, pure and light for the divine words. Worldly food is, then, the former life and sins; but the divine food is faith, hope, love, patience, knowledge, peace, temperance."

— Theodotus, *Selections from the Prophetic Scriptures*

"But let not your fasts be with the hypocrites; for they fast on the second and fifth day of the week; but you fast on the fourth day and the Preparation (Friday)."

— Polycarp, *The Teaching of the Twelve Apostles*

"But before the baptism let the baptizer fast, and be baptized, and whatever others can; but you shall order the baptized to fast one or two days before the others."

— Polycarp, *The Teaching of the Twelve Apostles*

"Prior to baptism, both he who is being baptized and he who is baptizing should fast, along with any others who can. And be sure the one who is baptized fasts for one or two days beforehand."

— *Didache*

"Fast to God in this way. Do nothing evil in your life, but serve the Lord with a clean heart, following his commandments and following his orders, and let no evil desire arise in your heart. Believe in God, because if you do these things and fear him and abstain from every evil deed, you will live to God. And if you do these things, you will complete a fast that is great and acceptable to the Lord."

— Hermas, *The Shepherd of Hermas*

"Behold, this is the fast I have chosen, says the Lord. Release the downtrodden with forgiveness, untie the knots of forcibly extracted agreements. Release the downtrodden with forgiveness, and tear up every unjust contract. Distribute your food to the hungry, and if you see someone naked, clothe him. Bring the homeless into your home, and if you see someone of lowly estate do not despise him."

— Barnabas, *The Letter of Barnabas*

"Those who are persuaded and believe that the things we teach and say are true, and promise that they live accordingly, are instructed to pray and beseech God with fasting for the remission of their past sins, while we pray and fast along with them."

— Justin Martyr, *The First Apology*

When You Fast

Read Matthew 17:14–21. What does verse twenty-one mean?

Has fasting been a part of your spiritual journey?

Why have so many Christians and churches been silent on this subject?

What is the right and the wrong way to fast?

What might you fast from aside from food?

How might you start becoming more involved in this spiritual discipline? (Richard Foster's book, *Celebration of Discipline*, has an excellent chapter on fasting.)

Treasures in Heaven

Do not store up for yourselves treasures on earth, where moth and rust destroy, and where thieves break in and steal. But store up for yourselves treasures in heaven, where moth and rust do not destroy, and where thieves do not break in and steal. For where your treasure is, there your heart will be also.

The eye is the lamp of the body. If your eyes are good, your whole body will be full of light. But if your eyes are bad, your whole body will be full of darkness. If then the light within you is darkness, how great is that darkness.

No one can serve two masters. Either he will hate the one and love the other, or he will be devoted to one and despise the other. You cannot serve both God and money.

—Matthew 6:19–24

Earlier in Matthew 6, Jesus has instructed his followers how to give, pray, and fast "in secret." Now, Jesus deals with the material things of this world. How we use our material things determines how our spiritual life turns out.

Early Christianity stressed simple, godly living. Private property was not forbidden, but it was to be used in the right way. Our things can curse us if we hoard them, or bless us if we share them with others.

"But those whom you consider rich, who add forests to forests, stretch out their fields far and wide into space without limbs, who possess immense sums of money, either in built-up heaps or in buried stores,—even in the midst of their riches those are torn to pieces by the anxiety of vague thoughts, lest the robber should spoil, lest the murderer should attack, lest the envy of some wealthier neighbor should become hostile, and harass them with malicious lawsuits. Such a one enjoys no security either in his food or his sleep. In the midst of the banquet he sights, although

44

he drinks from a jeweled goblet; and when his luxurious bed has enfolded his body, languid from feasting, he lies wakeful in the midst of the down; nor does he perceive, poor wretch, that these things are merely gilded torments, that he is held bondage by his gold, and that he is the slave of his luxury and wealth rather than their master. From him there is no liberality to dependents, no communication to the poor."

— Cyprian, *The Epistles of Cyprian*

"For if no one had anything, what room would be left among men for giving? And how can this dogma fail to be found plainly opposed to and conflicting with many other excellent teachings of the Lord? 'Make to yourself friends with the mammon of unrighteousness, that when you fail, they may receive you into the everlasting habitations.' 'Acquire treasures in heaven, whether neither moth nor rust destroy, nor thieves bread through.' How could one give food to the hungry, and drink to the thirsty, clothe the naked, and shelter the homeless, for not doing which He threatens with fire and outer darkness, if each man first divested himself of all these things?"

— Clement of Alexandria, *Who Is the Rich Man That Shall Be Saved?*

"Riches, then, which benefit also our neighbours, are not to be thrown away. For they are possessions, inasmuch as they are possessed, and goods, inasmuch as they are useful and provided by God for the use of men; and they lie to our hand, and are put under our power, as material and instruments which are for good use to those who know the instrument. If you use it skillfully, it is skillful; if you are deficient in skill, it is affected by your want or skill, being itself destitute of blame. Such an instrument is wealth. Are you able to make a right use of it?"

— Clement of Alexandria, *Who Is the Rich Man That Shall Be Saved?*

"For we ourselves, besides our attention to the word of Gospel, do not neglect our inferior employments. Some of us are fishermen, some tentmakers, some husbandmen, that we never are idle . . . For the Lord our God hates the slothful. For no one of those who are dedicated to God ought to be idle."

— *Constitutions of the Holy Apostles*

"Instead of lands, therefore, buy afflicted souls, according as each one is able, and visit widows and orphans and do not overlook them; spend your wealth and all your preparations which you received from the Lord, upon such lands and houses. For to this end did the Master make you rich, that you might perform services to him."

— Hermas, *The Shepherd of Hermas*

"The Lord ate from a common bowl, and made the disciples recline on the grass on the ground, and washed their feet, birded with a linen towel — He, the lowly minded God, and the Lord of the universe. He did not bring down a silver foot-bath from heaven. He asked to drink of the Samaritan woman, who drew the water from the well in an earthenware vessel, not seeking regal gold, but teaching us how to quench thirst easily. For he made use, not extravagance His aim."

"For luxury is prone to kick up its heels and toss its mane, and shake off the charioteer, the Instructor; who, pulling back the reins from far, leads and drives to salvation the human horse—that is, the irrational part of the soul—which is wildly bent on pleasures, and vicious appetites, and precious stones, and gold, and variety of dress, and other luxuries."

"Wealth seems to me to be like a serpent, which will twist round the hand and bite; unless one knows how to lay hold of it without danger by the point of the tail. And riches, wriggling in an experienced or inexperienced grasp, are dexterous at adhering and biting; unless one, despising them, use them skillfully, so as to crush the creature by the charm of the Word, and himself escape unscathed."

> — Clement of Alexandria on simple
> living, from *The Instructor*

Treasures in Heaven

How can we live in a simple and uncluttered way?

How can we view our material things in a Christian way?

What are less important things that demand too much attention in our lives?

What do verses twenty-two and twenty-three mean?

Where is your own treasure?

How important are your material things to you?

How do you use your leisure time to further God's kingdom?

Do Not Worry

Therefore I tell you, do not worry about your life, what you will eat or drink; or about your body, what you will wear. Is not life more important than food, and the body more important than clothes? Look at the birds of the air; they do not sow or reap or store away in barns, and yet your heavenly Father feeds them. Are you not much more valuable than they? Who of you by worrying can add a single hour to his life?

And why do you worry about clothes? See how the lilies of the field grow. They do not labor or spin. Yet I tell you that not even Solomon in all his splendor was dressed like one of these. If that is how God clothes the grass of the field, which is here today and tomorrow is thrown into the fire, will he not much more clothe you, O you of little faith? So do not worry, saying, 'What shall we eat?' or 'What shall we drink?' For the pagans run after all these things, and your heavenly Father knows that you need them. But seek first after his kingdom and his righteousness, and all these things will be given to you as well. Therefore do not worry about tomorrow, for tomorrow will worry about itself. Each day has enough trouble of its own.

—Matthew 6:25–34

The Greek word we translate "anxious" comes from two words meaning "to divide" and "the mind." When we worry, our mind is divided. Someone wrote, "Worry is a small trickle of fear that cuts through our mind until it cuts a channel into which all other thoughts are drained." Kierkegaard once said, "No Grand Inquisitor has in readiness such terrible torture as anxiety."

In our text, Jesus gives us a number of arguments against worry. Early Christianity stressed simple living, which cut down on things to worry about and centered life.

"Having therefore convinced us in the former time that our nature was unable to attain life, and having now revealed the Saviour who is able to save even those things which it was formerly impossible to save, by both these facts he desired to lead us to trust in His kindness, to esteem Him as our Nourisher, Father, Teacher, Counselor, Healer, our Wisdom, Light, Honour, Glory, Power, and Life, so that we should not be anxious concerning clothing and food."

— Mathetes, *The Epistle to Diognetus*

"For there is one God who feeds the fowls and the fishes, and in a word, the irrational creatures, and not one thing whatever is wanting to them, though 'they take no thought for their food.' And we better than they, being their lords, and more closely allied to God, as being wiser; and we were made, not that we might eat or drink, but that we might devote ourselves to the knowledge of God."

— Clement of Alexandria, *The Instructor*

"Since you, therefore enjoy such a providential care from Him, you ought to return praise to Him that receives the orphan and the widow."

— Tertullian, *On Idolatry*

"Does not he, who denies the Lord, deny himself? For does he not rob his Master of His authority, who deprives himself of his relationship to Him? He, then, who denies the Saviour, denies life; for 'the light was life.' He does not term those men of little faith, but faithless and hypocrites, who have the name inscribed on them, but deny that they are really believers."

— Clement of Alexandria, *The Stromata*

"It demonstrated to us, that both 'dear pledges,' and handicrafts and trades, are to be quite left behind for the Lord's sake, while James and John, called up by the Lord, do leave quite behind both father and ship; while Matthew is roused from the tollbooth; while even burying his father was too tardy a business for faith. None of them whom the Lord chose to him said, 'I have no means to live.' Faith fears not famine."

— Tertullian, *On Idolatry*

"To those who seek God's kingdom and righteousness, He promises that all things shall be added. For since all things are God's, nothing will be wanting to him who possesses God . . . Thus a meal was divinely provided for Daniel; when he was shut up by the king's command in the den of lions, and in the midst of wild beasts who were hungry, and yet spared him, the man of God was fed. Thus Elijah in his flight was nourished by ravens ministering to him in his solitude, and by birds bringing him food in his persecution."

— Cyprian, *The Treatises of Cyprian*

"But that which is squandered on foolish lusts is to be reckoned waste, not expenditure. For God has given to us, I know well, the liberty of use, but only so far as necessary; and He has determined that the use should be common. And it is monstrous for one to live in luxury, while many are in want. How much more glorious is it to do good to many, than to live sumptuously! How much wiser to spend money on human beings, than jewels and gold! How much more useful to acquire decorous friends, than lifeless ornaments!"

— Clement of Alexandria, *The Instructor*

"For it is shown in scripture, 'Take no thought what things you shall eat, or what you shall drink.' For to take thought of these things argues greed and luxury. Now eating, considered merely by itself, is a sign of necessity, repletion, as we have said, or want. Whatever is beyond that is a sign of superfluity. And what is superfluous, Scripture declares to be of the devil . . . The nations are dissolute and foolish. And what are the things he specifies? Luxury, voluptuousness, rich cooking, dainty feeding, gluttony."

— Clement of Alexandria, *The Instructor*

Do Not Worry

What do you worry about the most?

What are other worries in your life?

What reasons for not worrying are given in the text?

Can you find times when God has intervened in your life to solve your worries?

When has God given you unexpected things or help?

Why are we so prone to deal with either our past or our future?

What is the relationship between trusting Christ as our Savior and trusting him for our daily needs?

What are steps you can take to eliminate needless worry in your life?

How can your life be more focused in following Christ?

Judging Others

Do not judge, or you too will be judged. For in the same way you judge others, you will be judged, and with the measure you use, it will be measured to you.

Why do you look at the speck of sawdust in your brother's eye and pay no attention to the plank in your own eye? How can you say to your brother, 'Let me take the speck out of your eye,' when all the time there is a plank in your own eye? You hypocrite, first take the plank out of your own eye, and then you will see clearly to remove the speck from your brother's eye.

Do not give to dogs what is sacred; do not throw your pearls to pigs. If you do, they may trample them under their feet, and then turn and tear you to pieces.

—Matthew 7:1–6

Our final chapter in the Sermon on the Mount deals with the Christian and his relationships. Jesus has already dealt with the Christian's character, influence, righteousness, piety, and ambition. Verses one to five deal with our relationship to others, with verse six warning us against sharing deeply with unsuitable individuals. Verses seven to eleven are concerned with relating to God. We then come to the climax and the conclusion of Christ's Sermon on the Mount.

Jesus forbids the judgement of others. If we are concerned about change, we need simply to look at ourselves.

"When he says, 'Judge not, lest you be judged,' does He not require patience? For who will refrain from judging another, but the patient person who seeks no revenge. We should only judge in order to pardon."
— Tertullian, *On Patience*

"We should ask that our debts be forgiven us in such a manner as we ourselves forgive our debtors, knowing that which we seek for our sins cannot be obtained unless we ourselves have acted in a similiar way in respect of our debtors. Therefore also he says in another place, 'With what measure you mete, it shall be measured to you.' And the servant who, after having all of his debt forgiven him by his master, would not forgive his fellow servant, is cast back into prison; because he would not forgive his fellow servant, he lost the indulgence that had been shown to himself by the Lord."

— Cyprian, *The Treatises of Cyprian*

Quotes regarding verse six:
"But let no one eat or drink of your Eucharist, but they who have been baptized into the name of the Lord, for concerning this also the Lord has said, 'Give not that which is holy to the dogs.'"

— Polycarp, *The Teaching of the Twelve Apostles*

"Baptism is not rashly to be administered . . . On the contrary, this precept is rather to looked at carefully: 'Give not the holy things to the dogs, nor cast your pearls before swine.'"

— Clement of Alexandria, *The Stromata*

"For it is difficult to exhibit the really pure and transparent words respecting the true light, to swinish and untrained hearers."

— Clement of Alexandria, *The Stromata*

Judging Others

Can you recall some dream or trait you had that was squelched by criticism? What might you do to recover it?

Think of a person who is judgemental. Why is that person that way, and not wise or discerning?

What is the difference between judgement and discernment?

Why is it so easy to judge others?

Why are we sometimes blind to our own faults?

What are the "specks of sawdust" or "planks" Jesus mentions?

How will our judgement of others affect us?

Can you think of examples of that in your own life?

Are there times when you wished you hadn't shared certain things with others?

How can the church practice discipline in the correct Christian manner?

Ask, Seek, Knock

Ask and it will be given to you; seek and you will find; knock and the door will be opened to you. For everyone who asks receives; he who seeks finds; and to him who knocks, the door will be opened.

Which of you, if his son asks for bread, will give him a stone? Or if he asks for a fish, will give him a snake? If you, then, though you are evil, know how to give good gifts to your children, how much more will your Father in heaven give good gifts to those who ask him! In everything, do to others what you would have them do to you, for this sums up the Law and the Prophets.

—Matthew 7:7–12

When we think of prayers of petition, we often ask God for various things. We want health, to be employed, to have sound homes and families. The early Christians often prayed for spiritual maturity and for a knowledge of how to serve God in the best way.

"Accordingly, good things are possessed by Christians alone. And nothing is richer than these good things; therefore these alone are rich. For righteousness is true riches; and the Word is more valuable than all treasures, not accruing from cattle and fields, but given by God—riches which cannot be taken away."

— Clement of Alexandria, *The Stromata*

Ask, Seek, Knock

What are the verbs in verse seven, and how are they used?

Are there limits to what we can ask God for?

Have there been times in your life when unanswered prayer was the best thing?

Based on what we have already learned in the Sermon on the Mount, what are things that we should ask for?

Why are your prayers sometimes unanswered?

What are things that you could ask, seek, and knock for?

The Narrow and Wide Gates

Enter through the narrow gate. For wide is the gate and broad is the road that leads to destruction, and many enter through it. But small is the gate and narrow the road that leads to life, and only a few find it.

—Matthew 7:13–14

Many scholars see this passage as being the start of the conclusion of the Sermon on the Mount. In this and the following section, Jesus gives choices. You must choose between broad and narrow ways, false and true teachers, verbal profession or radical discipleship, a foundation of sand verses that of rock.

Christianity for the early Christians was a great journey, starting at the time of baptism and ending at the gates of heaven. A true disciple would find both great joy and great hardship along the way.

"You read how broad is the road to evil, how thronged in comparison with the opposite: would not all glide down the road if there were nothing in it to fear? We dread the Creator's tremendous threats, and yet scarcely turn away from evil."

— Tertullian, *Against Marcion*

"For the narrow way is the gate of heaven; and this is a house of God, where the Good Diety dwells alone. And into this gate he says, no unclean person shall enter, nor one that is natural or carnal; but it is reserved for the spiritual only."

— Hippolytus, *The Refutation of All Heresy*

"There are two ways, one of life and one of death; but a great difference between the two ways. The way of life then, is this: First, you shall love

God, who made you; second, your neighbor as yourself; and all things that you would not want to occur to you, do not do to another."

— Polycarp, *The Teaching of the Twelve Apostles*

"Before virtue is placed exertion, and long and steep is the way to it, and rough at first; but when the summit is reached, then it is easy, though difficult before."

— Clement of Alexandria, *The Stromata*

The Narrow and Wide Gates

Which decisions and actions are the hardest for you?

Why do we normally choose the easy way in life?

What must you leave behind if you go through the narrow gate?

How can our witnessing to others include the concept of the narrow gate?

A Tree and Its Fruit

Watch out for false prophets. They come to you in sheep's clothing, but inwardly they are ferocious wolves. By their fruit you will recognize them. Do people pick grapes from thornbushes, or figs from thistles? Likewise every good tree bears good fruit, but a bad tree bears bad fruit. A good tree cannot bear bad fruit, and a bad tree cannot bear good fruit. Every tree that does not bear good fruit is cut down and thrown into the fire. Thus, by their fruit you will recognize them.

Not everyone who says to me, 'Lord, Lord,' will enter the kingdom of heaven, but only he who does the will of my father in heaven. Many will say to me on that day, 'Lord, Lord,' did we not prophesy in your name, and in your name drive out demons and perform miracles? Then I will tell them plainly, 'I never knew you. Away from me, you evildoers!'

—Matthew 7:15–23

The prophets in the Old Testament dressed a certain way, wearing a sheepskin mantle. Anyone could dress that way, fooling the unaware. In the time of the early church, many claimed to be true prophets when in reality they were false ones. This same problem is still with us today.

"Whoever, therefore, comes and teaches you all these things that have been said before, receive him. But if the teacher turns and teaches another doctrine to the destruction of this, hear him not; but if he teaches so as to increase righteousness and the knowledge of the Lord, receive him as the Lord. Let every apostle that comes to you be received as the Lord. But he shall not remain except one day; but if there be need, also the next; but if he remains three days, he is a false prophet."

— Polycarp, *The Teaching of the Twelve Apostles*

"There are, therefore, and there were many, my friends, who coming forward in the name of Jesus, taught both to speak and act impious and blasphemous things; and these are called by us after the name of the men from whom each doctrine and opinion had its origin . . . Some are called Marcians, and some Basilidians, and some Saturnilians, and others by other names; each called after the originator of the individual opinion, just as one of those who consider themselves philosophers thinks he must bear the name of the philosophy which he follows, from the name of the father of the particular doctrine."

> — Justin Martyr, *Dialogue with Trypho*

"Avoid those who under the name of Christ and Moses, war against Christ and Moses, and in the clothing of the sheep hide the wolf. For these are the false Christs, and false prophets, and false apostles, deceivers and corrupters, portions of foxes, the destroyers of the herbs of the vineyards."

> — *Constitutions of the Holy Apostles*

A Tree and Its Fruit

What do verses twenty-one and twenty-two tell us about the appearance of false prophets?

How do we recognize the conflict between identifying false prophets and not judging?

How do we recognize and confront the sin in our own lives?

Who might be false prophets in the church today?

Why is it so important to have integrity and accountability built into our church structures today?

Why isn't a verbal profession of faith in Christ enough?

Do the Will of God

Not everyone who says to me, 'Lord, Lord,' will enter the kingdom of heaven, but only he who does the will of my Father who is in heaven. Many will say to me on that day, 'Lord, Lord, did we not prophesy in your name, and in your name drive our demons and perform many miracles? Then I will tell them plainly, 'I never knew you. Away from me, you evildoers!'

Therefore everyone who hears these words of mine and puts them into practice is like a wise man who built his house on the rock. The rain came down, the streams rose, and the winds blew, and beat against that house; yet it did not fall, because it had its foundation on the rock. But everyone who hears these words of mine and does not put them into practice is like a foolish man who built his house on the sand. The rain came down, the streams rose, and the winds blew and beat against that house, and it fell with a great crash.

—Matthew 7:24–27

Making God the center of our lives is the Christian's goal. In our age, we often find ourselves trapped by wanting to use God. We ask, "How can God help me?" "Will this be useful to me?" Yet Jesus calls us to follow him in obedience, and to live out his teachings in our daily lives.

If we look back at early Christianity, we see great power connected with great obedience. In spite of the fact that the people were simple and often ignorant of the Bible—for manuscripts were only rarely possessed by individuals—and in spite of the newness of their faith and the deep influence of their old pagan customs, their spiritual life and their demonstration of obedience and zeal were fine examples of life lived under the precepts of the Gospel.

The early Christians lived by what they heard. Commandments fell on faithful hearts that were ready to obey. Christ's words entered deeply into daily Christian life, and the Gospel was translated into obedient living. The Gospel was a way of living, and it was far more than an intellectual system to be discussed and analyzed. Today faithful followers of Christ can still draw life for themselves from the living spring of the understanding of Christianity by those who lived the closest to its source.

As we approach the third millenium of Christianity, a returning to our own roots has the power to guide and instruct us in God's way of living.

"And let those who are not found living as He taught, be understood to be not Christians, even though they profess with the lip the precepts of Christ; for not those who make profession, but those who do the works, shall be saved, according to his word: 'Not every one who saith to Me, Lord, Lord, shall enter the kingdom of heaven, but he that doeth the will of my Father which is in heaven.' . . . And as to those who are not living pursuant to these His teachings, and are Christians only in name, we demand that such be punished by you."

— Justin Martyr, *The First Apology*

"Let us then, not only call Him Lord, for that will not save us. For He saith, 'Not every one that saith to Me, Lord, Lord, shall be saved, but he that works righteousness.' Wherefore, brethren, let us confess Him by our works, by loving another, by not committing adultery, or speaking evil of one another, or cherishing envy; but being content, compassionate, and good."

— Clement, *II Clement*

"'Whoever,' says He, 'Heareth my words, and doeth them, I will liken him unto a wise man, that built his house upon a rock: the rain descended, the floods came, the winds blew, and beat upon that house; and it fell not: for it was rounded upon a rock.' We ought therefore to stand fast on His words, to learn and do whatever He both taught and did. But how can a man say that he believes in Christ, who does not do what Christ commanded him to do? Or whence shall he attain the reward of faith, who will not keep the faith of commandment? He must of necessity wander, and caught away by a spirit of error, like dust which is shaken by the wind, be blown apart; and he will make no advance towards salvation, because he does not keep the truth of salvation."

— Cyprian, *The Epistles of Cyprian*

Do the Will of God

What changes will you make in your life as a result of this study?

What have you learned new since starting your journey into the Sermon on the Mount?

In what areas is it hard for you to obey the Sermon on the Mount?

Should new converts be taught the faith of the Sermon on the Mount?

How will Jesus have a new authority over you in concluding this study?

How will you depend upon God in helping you grow in faith and obedience?

Appendix: Early Christian Writers and Documents

Clement of Alexandria. Clement was a philosopher who discovered Christ while on a journey in search of spiritual truth. After his conversion, he traveled extensively to learn about his new faith. He eventually settled in Alexandria, Egypt, and helped to establish that city as a key center of learning and scholarship for the early Christian church. Although his writings are dated from about 190 A.D. until his death in 215 or 216 A.D., Clement claimed that those he studied under were directly influenced by Christ's apostles.

Clement of Rome. Of the writers in this appendix, Clement of Rome is the only one to be mentioned in scripture. (See Philippians 4:2.) He lived from approximately 30 to 100 A.D. Iranaeus, writing in the last third of the second century, identifies him as the bishop of Rome from 92 to 101 A.D. The Roman Catholic Church lists him as the fourth bishop of Rome, making him the fourth pope. His most famous work is a letter addressed to a Corinthian church in response to some young men usurping the authority of the church's rightful leaders. He argues that church authority and structure is ordained by God, and that love should be the key to the solution. Those in rebellion are counseled to repent and submit to the proper authority. For centuries thereafter, many Christian authors quoted from Clement, some even including his letter in lists of New Testament books.

Cyprian. Cyprian was a wealthy Roman who converted to Christianity at the age of forty. So enthusiastic was he about the new religion that he liquidated his entire estate and gave the money to the poor. He rejoiced in his act, and his writings contain the joy of his conversion. The church at Carthage in North Africa elected him to be a bishop even though he had been a Christian for only a few years. His writings are especially valuable because they consist chiefly of correspondence with the leaders of other churches, revealing the everyday concerns and problems of early Christianity. During his ten-year tenure as bishop, he guided the church through the Decian persecution and a fearful plague. During a period of inner turmoil in the church, he devoted much of his energy to maintaining church unity. He was martyred in 258 A.D.

Didache. Although the exact authorship and date of this document is not firmly established, it was probably produced between 90 and 120 A.D., either in Egypt or Syria. Rediscovered by a scholar in 1873 who was studying at a monastery in Constantinople, it is a priceless piece of Christian literature which was revered by church leaders up through the fourth century. Athanasius, the fourth century bishop of Alexandria, recommended it for new converts. The text includes instructions dealing with food, baptism, prayer, fasting, and communion; indeed, the document offers a detailed view of a very early Christian community. The text is also important for its influence on later documents like *The Teachings of the Twelve Apostles* and the *Apostolic Tradition*.

Ignatius of Antioch. When we think of early Christianity, we think of martyrdom. Ignatius brings to us a powerful message of what it means. "Let me be food for the wild beasts, through which I can attain to God. I am the wheat of God and I am ground by the teeth of wild beasts so that I may be found the pure bread of Christ. Instead, entice the wild beasts so that they may become my tomb and leave no trace of my body, so that when I fall asleep I may not burden anyone. Then I shall be truly a disciple of Christ." When we encounter Ignatius, he is already doomed to death, a convict in chains guarded by ten Roman soldiers, making his way from Antioch, the place of his bishopric, to the amphitheater in Rome, where he was martyred in 107 A.D. During two pauses of his journey, he wrote seven letters, full of various warnings, solemn exaltations, and the passionate desire to simultaneously live to proclaim Christ and to die for him. His letters are passionate and blunt, full of emotion and courage. Tradition has it that Ignatius was a disciple of John, and that Paul ordained him to care for Gentile converts in Antioch. He became the second bishop of Antioch, the city in Syria from which Barnabas and Paul set out on their famous missionary journey.

Justin Martyr. As a young man in pursuit of truth, Justin had been dissatisfied with the various schools of Greek philosophy. Converted by an old man to Christianity, he continued to wear his philosopher's robe to symbolize that he had found the one true philosophy. Journeying from Palestine to

Rome, he dedicated his life to educating Romans about the meaning of Christianity. Justin's written defenses of Christianity to the Romans are the oldest Christian apologies in existence. They converted many Romans, learned and unlearned alike. In the end, a group of philosophers plotted against him and had him arrested. Choosing to die rather than give up his faith, Justin was executed about 165 A.D. After his death, he became known as Justin the Martyr, or simply Justin Martyr.

Polycarp of Smyrna. Encouraged by a proconsul to revile Christ to save his life, Polycarp's response was direct and to the point: "I have served Him eighty-six years and in no way has He dealt unjustly with me; so how can I blaspheme my King who saved me?" Polycarp had to fully understand that his response meant martyrdom. On a day in February 156 A.D., he was burned to death before a vast stadium crowd. He had lived a long and productive life. He was a personal disciple and companion of the apostle John. For some fifty years, he served as bishop of the church at Smyrna, one of the seven churches mentioned in the first part of Revelation. Although only one letter by Polycarp survives, a letter to the church at Philipi, this letter is filled with quotations from the Gospels, Acts, the Epistles, as well as the letters of Clement and Ignatius. In Polycarp, we have a link to the earliest days of Christianity.

Shepherd of Hermas. Believed to have been written between 100 and 150 A.D., probably in Rome, this text was widely known. Iranaeus and Tertullian both make reference to it. Its central theme is repentance. To quote directly: "To repent is great understanding. For the one who sins understands that he has done evil before the Lord, and the deed which he has done rises up in his heart, and he repents and no longer commits the evil deed, but does good deeds all the more and humbles and torments his own soul because he has sinned. So you see repentance is great understanding." The text emphasizes the tension between God's standards and his mercy, but the author of *The Shepherd* has little patience with impurity in the church.

Tertullian. Tertullian is perhaps the best known of the early Christian writers. A leader in the North African church at Carthage, he wrote his works in Latin rather than Greek during a span from roughly 190 to 210 A.D. He is known for several memorable sayings, such as "The blood of the martyrs is the seed of the church." Although he was a defender of orthodoxy against the heresies of the day, writing apologetic works and exhorting Christians to maintain their separation from the world, late in life he joined the Montanist sect. This sect was orthodox in theology, but it expected its members to follow man-made ascetic commands.